homecoming

DREAMING BIG in a small town

a collection of essays by

Krisha Chachra

homecoming Journals
DREAMING BIG in a small town

Entire Contents Copyright © 2007 Krisha Chachra
All Rights Reserved
No part of this book may be reproduced in any form without written permission from the author

Articles are reprinted with the permission of the Roanoke Times, www.roanoke.com
Copyright © the Roanoke Times, 2002-2004

Photos by JD Vogt and Krisha Chachra
Editing by Deirdre Jain

Book design by Mountain Trail Press LLC
www.mountaintrailpress.com

ISBN-13: 978-1-4243-2921-2
ISBN-10: 1-4243-2921-3
Printed in Korea
First Printing, Spring 2007

When people ask me why on earth I live in Blacksburg, Virginia, I tell them 'because I figured out a way to stay here.' And for those of you who are lucky enough to call a small town your home, you understand what I mean. Returning home is always a story that must somehow be explained. The mind spends a lifetime plotting to leave, but the heart longs for a lifestyle only had by returning. These are stories of rediscovering the wide-open spaces and slower pace of my Southwestern Virginia hometown after thriving on the energy of an upbeat and upscale life in the nation's capital at the turn of the millennium. As a first generation Indian-American, my goal was always to leave the Appalachian Mountains and escape to the city to find fresh ideas and diverse perspectives. After September 11, 2001, Washington D.C. offered no more opportunity for me. So with secret shame, I came back home. I learned, however, that there was nothing to be ashamed of. In time, I discovered that a small hometown is built on a mighty support system. I learned that a community is much like a free space on a bingo card: you know as long as you have one, you're a step closer to winning.

These are your stories too: the stories of people who make changes in their lives by returning to a place where memories and experiences materialize as sharply as the day they were made. A place called home where nothing has really changed. Nothing, except for the way you see it.

– Krisha Chachra, 2007

"Home is the place where, when you have to go there,
They have to take you in."
– Robert Frost

Special Thanks

to my community: the people who make up the character of this town, those involved in our civic, local, volunteer and government organizations who give their time and their hearts making this a special place to live. Those who have always encouraged me to keep writing, use my voice and believe in the power of the written word. Anyone who has lived in our town, for any period of time, and spreads the gospel of our true beauty. Our long time friends and our colleagues at Virginia Tech who have stood by my family and me and have shared our successes. My personal friends who have been my supporters and teachers. My teachers who have been my inspiration. My inspiration, that comes from the example of three people who have stood unshakably by my side my entire life.

Contents

Memories Sold on the Auction Block	8
New Attitude Brings Appreciation for Hometown	10
Taking a Trip Down Memory Lane with BHS Alums	14
Looking for Love in All the Right Places	18
Depending on Local Connections in a Shrinking Global Village	20
Becoming an American, a Journey of Opportunity and Sacrifice	22
Finding Your Dreams Where You Live	24
Find Your Own Stories to Tell	26
Rain Makes Gardens, and Families, Grow?	30
Goodbye Summer, Hello Student Hoards	34
Driven to Distraction on I-81	36
Give Thanks for Family, Food, and Football	38
Blacksburg is Always Just a Memory Away	42
When the Past Emerges Out of the Soggy Present	44
Would Founding Family be Proud of this Town?	46
From My Shadow to My Friend	50
The Indians are Gathering for their 10th Reunion	54
Columnist Ready to Spread her Wings on the Big Island	56

Dedicated to those who dream big in small towns

Memories Sold on the Auction Block

AN AUCTION IS A STRANGE THING to witness. Bit by bit, chunks of unspoiled land, slices of residential property, historical landmarks and treasured possessions are sold, in a matter of minutes, to the highest bidder. One can't help feeling a little sad to see something so valuable – sentimental or otherwise – sold to strangers.

It can be sad, especially if the deal consists of someone else walking away with the heart of the hometown you grew up in.

Five hundred people packed in the Donaldson Brown Center to watch the sale of downtown Blacksburg and other HCMF property in Southwest Virginia. In total, all the property sold for close to $12.6 million, including a 5 percent buyer's premium. I, of course, had no chance of exceeding the Internet bidders, let alone the suited businessmen who had conducted months of research to turn their dollars into great investments. Like so many Blacksburg residents in the audience wearing "guest" badges, I was there to see the faces of the winners who would walk away with pieces of the town in which I was born 26 years ago.

"It is only money, you can't take it with you so bid aggressively," the auctioneer hollered.

But to me, most of "Sales 1–20" weren't just money, they were memories. One of my first childhood babysitters, an international student at Virginia Tech, lived in the apartment building that was Sale 1 on the auction block. She would let me sit out in the front yard and pick dandelions for her, never once informing me in endearing broken English that I was handing her a bunch of weeds. Sale 1, 403 Progress St., sold for $625,000. I wondered if the new owners planned to plant real flowers out front.

I did get my mother, who was sitting next to me, to bid on Sale 7 (just for fun), an offer that lasted about 15 seconds. The property, I remembered, was on the corner of Ellett and Fairfax roads. When I was younger, my parents used to take me to the long-since-gone Ipanema restaurant across from that corner. I recalled loving the look of that steep hill on Sale 7 (it looked a lot steeper then), which I envisioned would make the perfect place to log roll in the summer and sled in the winter.

I never got a chance to do either. And if the new owners level it off and build a multi-unit residential, which the property is zoned for, perhaps I never will.

But everyone was there to see who would win Sale 13. In the heart of downtown, the historical Lyric Theater has overcome her fair share of near-death experiences. Saved and now operated by the residents of Blacksburg, the Lyric changed hands on the auction block at least 15 times.

I remember when I was 9 years old I got to go see a movie there – by myself. I felt so grown up sitting in that big theater and so proud that I was allowed to go on my own, that I can't even recall what the movie was about.

A price war for the Lyric took the tag up 700 percent from its initial bid. It was good to see so many people recognized its value, both to the community and for the investment. In the end, the Lyric was grouped in with four other lots making up downtown Blacksburg. It all sold for $4.2 million to bidder No. 11. I didn't know who bidder 11 was, but they now owned an entire block of memories where thousands of people experienced something momentous at one time – meeting someone special at the Corner Drug, eating ice cream in Gillie's or hiding between the aisles in Books, Strings & Things. My parents' first apartment in Blacksburg, more than 30 years ago, was above what now is the Rivermill.

Even if the businesses varied over the years, the memories were always still there. And if the Lyric remains intact, I'll definitely go to the movies again. Alone.

I'm all for change. I think some new ownership can only breed interesting ideas, attract new business and keep Blacksburg moving forward. But still, if it was up to me, and I had $12.6 million, I would have bought a town. My hometown. And kept it exactly the way I remembered.

© The Roanoke Times, Sep. 8, 2002, www.roanoke.com, by Krisha Chachra

New Attitude Brings Appreciation for Hometown

There aren't many places where a 5-foot-11 Asian Indian can hide in these parts.

The haystacks in my Blacksburg back yard, although great perches for spying into the neighbor's barn, hardly provide full coverage from the townies passing by in Tacoma pickups.

And I can't pretend to window shop on Main Street downtown and get lost in the crowd. There's not enough crowd anymore, thanks to the mega-multiplex eight miles away.

Maybe I could escape to Floyd, where the general store hosts flatfooters and old-time musicians every Friday night, and sit quietly observing the serious faces of the cloggers. But then I would get asked to dance, and I'd have to use the steps I learned 15 years ago.

Once, however, a local interrupted my solitude not with "Care to dance?" but with "So, where ya from?" I wondered if I should give him the answer he really wanted. So I tested.

"I'm from here."

Looking a little awkward and confused, he re-checked my long black hair and dark complexion before pressing on: "No, where ya really from?" That's when I gave in, saying, "Oh!" and then a surprised, "I'm Indian!"

The local, pleased with the answer, rolled up his flannel shirt, exposing a well-developed forearm. Displaying a dream-catcher tattoo, he grinned and said proudly, "I'm part Cherokee, too!"

Suddenly, we were family.

So I don't try to hide anymore. There's no reason to. When you're an Indian from India and grow up in a small American town, as I did, you stand out.

But out of sheer necessity to bond you become a local, a member of the family, a country gal. You trade stories and trade cultures, just to get close with your community.

I think I'm the only 26-year-old Indian country girl alive fully equipped with a Southern accent and a tractor and living on a 70-acre farm.

And I love my life.

Eight years ago, I left Blacksburg for the big city, college and graduate school. Life was endless appointments and cocktail parties. It was pure excitement. And then things changed. When the glamour was over, I headed south, gravitating toward home. I was craving something familiar, something I could count on. But when I arrived I felt so isolated I wanted to hide.

Nothing had changed besides me.

Most of my high school friends had stayed and were now living their best lives, some of them having married their high-school sweethearts. The best entertainment was playing darts at smoky local hangouts and counting the fireflies from the porch swing. It was a little different than laughing quietly and sipping drinks at political fund-raisers. Sure, the town had grown, with more high-tech business and traffic now, but the community was the same.

And I wasn't.

Until, one day, I realized I was better off in the mountains than in the city. I don't know what made me change my mind. Maybe it was my best friend moving back to town. Or the fact that being negative just did not suit me. At any rate, I started giving small-town living a chance. I planned backyard barn parties and invited all my friends. I started listening to bluegrass music. I took long country walks.

I started to fit in, realizing that many people live their whole lives in a town and feel displaced. They don't know the cashier at Kroger or anything about the teller at the bank. They don't have that family connection with their town. That connection, the feeling of belonging, is not something a big city can offer.

This was my hometown. I didn't have to hide. It was all familiar.

Nothing had changed except my attitude.

I began to do the things that made me so happy at one time in this community. A community will not forget you as long as you remember you are part of it.

I am an Indian.
I am a country music fan.
I am a world traveler.
And I live on a farm.

It's amazing what you find out about yourself when you're back with family.

© The Roanoke Times, Nov. 26, 2002, www.roanoke.com, by Krisha Chachra

Taking a Trip Down Memory Lane with BHS Alums

It seems that no matter how far away they fly, flocks of Blacksburg High School graduates always swoop back into town for the holidays.

As the ancient Chinese mystic Lao Tsu once wrote, "Going on means going far, going far means returning," every year the 'locals from Christmas past' meet for an unplanned reunion at PK's or catch up at the Underground, two favorite community hideouts.

It was during one of these spontaneous gatherings that I heard my now-city-slicker friends complain that no matter how far they go and how long they stay away, Blacksburg never changes.

That's when I got slightly defensive and pointed out our concrete jungle tribute to development in the New River Valley. Change is everywhere – Triangle Lanes just shut down to make room for another Drugstore and we even built a bypass to skirt all the traffic.

But forget the expansion of the Mall; look at the big-time transformations that have happened right here in downtown Blacksburg, I tell them. McCoy funeral home moved to a new place about a mile away, and the old house it occupied has been moved across Draper Road to make room for a parking garage.

And then I tell them about a little game my best friend and I play when we're overseas and home-sick.

"Name all the things that used to be where Maria's café is now," one of us says. OK, it was The Coffee Pot, then some sort of T-shirt place, and of course, the Hawaii Kai. The corner of Main and College Ave.? Easy: Corner Drug.

Sharkey's? It was Cricket's, just down the street from the former Arnold's sub shop.

Baylee's? South Main Café.

Then everyone gets in on the game, recalling history bounded by twenty-something year old memories.

The basement next to the Record Exchange? Used to be The Hobbie Shop.

The top of the Cellar? Was it Winter Sun?

How about Pedro's? You're way behind buddy – it's been the Library and Waterstreet Café since you left town.

STA Travel? It was Council Travel after Blue Ridge Outdoors moved into Grand Piano's spot across from the Post Office downtown.

Hey, remember when Gillie's served ice cream?

And Diary Queen was the Fun 'N' Games store, not to be confused with the Beholder's Eye that is where King Video used to be. I still have King Video's membership card – or should I say Video Update – or wait! Movie Gallery now.

And what used to be in Movie Gallery's spot? A steakhouse. What was the name? Longhorn? Or was it Western Sizzlin'? No, that was where Bonomo's is now.

Now go to University Mall: Math Emporium? Roses, and before that, Woolco.

The Weight Club? Sydney's.

But that Chinese restaurant has outlasted them all.

What about Gables Shopping Center on the other side of town? Can anyone name all the restaurants before El Guadalupes?

Let's not go there.

I ask for my tab, just to learn that an old-timer, silently smiling in the corner, has paid for it. He probably enjoyed our festive recollection of how things used to be.

Maybe I can't get my haircut by Chau at Big Al's anymore or buy a novel at Books Strings & Things, but after I return from that far off place Lao Tsu speaks of, I know I can walk into Poor Billy's or the Rivermill and be welcomed by someone who knows me, this town and our history. My friends are correct. Some things never change in Blacksburg.

And rightly so.

Looking for Love in All the Right Places

So Congratulations.

You're smart, beautiful, young, fun, unattached (by choice, of course) and made it through another Valentine's Day.

For the last two months, you've managed to dodge the flying red romantic cards flung at you down every pharmacy aisle and keep from gaining 50 pounds by consuming discounted heart shaped candy you would normally buy for yourself. You are a single, young professional living in Blacksburg, and mostly you're fine with that. Well, except on national holidays.

According to Blacksburg's census data, there are about 5,000 people between the ages of 25 and 44, and 3,500 single-family households in this town. So, where are those people hiding?

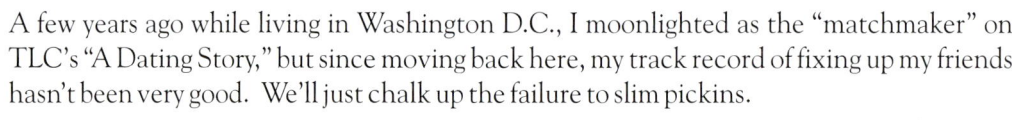

A few years ago while living in Washington D.C., I moonlighted as the "matchmaker" on TLC's "A Dating Story," but since moving back here, my track record of fixing up my friends hasn't been very good. We'll just chalk up the failure to slim pickins.

Blacksburg is supposed to be the most 'wired' town in America. Where is all the connectivity?

Maybe that's the problem. All the interesting singles live in chat rooms and trade emails instead of phone numbers. About 90 percent of Blacksburg residents have access to the Internet, so maybe I can redeem my reputation and find some new viable prospects online.

After searching "Singles in Blacksburg, Virginia," I get a few hits including www.nasingles.com/va/blacksburg-singles.htm. When I browse through the singles ages 25-35, it is like a splash page of people I'd lost touch with since high school. I find two of my fellow high school graduates, one bouncer I know from downtown and my optometrist. Then there are the mixed messages: a few people claim that 'brainiac' is a turn-off while they describe themselves as 'clever' or 'witty' –

nothing better than misunderstood razor-sharp repartee to get the ball rolling on a first date.

Maybe the real turn offs are tag lines people use as attention grabbers: "I love to melt plastic army men," or "Not-so-great looking girl, in need of male attention," or "Short one seeks big ole sweetie."

No luck there. At www.meetwithamate.com/dating/in/va/Blacksburg/ there is only one posting by "Marlin" who didn't even bother putting up a picture or a description of himself.

And that's the singles scene we are used to around here. As far as I can tell, the local single's itinerary consists of a whirlwind weekly tour of dart bars, pool halls and the random comedy night or all-you-can eat wings thrown in for variety.

But who is complaining, really? The best way to meet people you'll like is to do things you like to do. If downtown isn't your scene, then don't worry; you aren't doomed to boredom as a bachelor or a spinster forever. It just takes a little motivation. In the last two weeks I've met people by painting pottery, attending a reception for a Hollywood producer, listening to live jazz downtown, eating at two new restaurants, sipping sour apple martinis at Kabuki's happy hour, going to a flea market, attending an international chocolate tasting at the Clay Corner Inn, seeing a Spanish opera, going to a luncheon slide show at the Cranwell International Center – and I even managed to have a darn good Valentine's day, with a Valentine.

But I'm not sure that kind of effort will last to the next national holiday. At least there is still leftover discounted heart shaped candy.

Depending on Local Connections in a Shrinking Global Village

As we all know, the world has shrunk to a global village. But we still depend on our local connections – perhaps now more than ever – for support and solidarity.

Here in our own village of Blacksburg, many of us find our connections in social and civic organizations – the groups that can reconnect us with people from our past and introduce us to new opportunities for the future.

Every once in a while I have an urge to escape, to find some wide-open spaces, so I take a lunch break and head to the Cranwell International Center. Every Wednesday at noon, volunteers share a slide show of their personal travel or work experiences. A couple of weeks ago my grade school friend's father was presenting his show about Africa. The slides were flavorful, but more fulfilling was finding out that my friend was now married and had a family. We're back in touch again, after fifteen years.

Our local chapter of the YMCA keeps the community active by offering inviting courses that pique any interest. When I returned to this area after living away a few years, these courses offered opportunities for me to finally discover art forms that I had always been curious about but never had the time to learn. I took pottery and soap making classes – and instantly had homemade holiday presents for all the important people in my personal community.

My friend finally got me to a "body pump" class at New Town Fitness last year, and our instructor, who didn't even break a sweat during the hour of exhaustion, turned out to also be the president of the board of directors of the Montgomery, Radford and Floyd United Way Chapter. If I'd never tried to build muscle, I might never have linked with the United Way or learned how important this organization was to our community.

But coincidental connections don't always lead to community involvement. Intentionally joining a group can better ensure you'll meet people with shared aims. While living in Washington, D.C., I belonged to an organization called the D.C. Young Professionals. Our activities helped connect young, ambitious individuals with others that had common interest. Now a handful of bright 20 and 30-somethings have created a similar organization in Blacksburg. The New River Nucleus currently meets on the first Thursday of the month at the Nerv. This hip happening may provide a fun atmosphere for people to connect with a new community of friends and also learn about local charitable organizations.

If you can't join the community or donate your time, maybe you can donate resources so that our village continues to thrive. You may know about a philanthropic organization called the Community Foundation of the New River Valley. The foundation makes grants to projects, groups and organization that address evolving needs in the community. In the past, donations have helped start a summer reading program for low-income children and have provided the means to build a greenhouse where at-risk teens could grow plants to sell at area farmer's markets.

These are only a few of the organizations that make up our community. They give us our identity and join us with others who have shared values, similar interests and a common history. It is through our community that we are connected in this small corner of the global village.

© The Roanoke Times, Mar. 25, 2003, www.roanoke.com, by Krisha Chachra

Becoming an American, a Journey of Opportunity and Sacrifice

I was around five years old when my mother swore her allegiance to the United States of America. The only thing I remember is sitting quietly on a long courtroom bench looking up from the string tied to my wrist. Floating happily above me was a small yellow balloon I received when entering the room. As my mother stood among a crowd of foreign faces and raised her right hand, I must have been just as proud to be there. After all, she was becoming an American citizen, and I had just scored the coolest yellow balloon in town.

Until now, I had never really asked my mom, or my dad for that matter, what becoming a citizen of this country felt like. For me, being part of this country had always been part of my life. Nothing I had to apply for, nothing I had to prove, nothing I even thought about – just something I was born with.

Thinking about it now, I can imagine naturalization is somewhat like being adopted – or maybe the word is accepted. Life doesn't change, but all of a sudden you feel more like you have a place at the table, like you're standing inside the circle, playing on the team and feeling part of a family. Suddenly everything you worked for, everything you left behind – including the relatives in your native country – everything you've sacrificed, has been worth it. With a simple certificate you feel validated. And you feel, as my parents told me, empowered to go forth without hesitation to meet the opportunity you traveled thousands of miles to seize. Really, it is a staggering experience.

For many of us, free time in Blacksburg is spent in the context of local bars and dart leagues or with family and friends in cozy living rooms occupied by board games and good conversation. Sometimes, we can't fully comprehend the sacrifice our immigrant neighbors have made just to buy the lot next to us or see their children educated.

Yes, we all make sacrifices and hard choices to move forward. But in order to receive the entire package of benefits and opportunities of American citizenship, imagine the critical sacrifice of renouncing allegiance to your native country. For some, it is probably an easy choice. Naturalization is the next step in a living dream that already includes an American education, an American salary, American children and an American way of life. For others, it is about survival, security, and escape from a dead-end and sometimes brutal future.

It is harder than you would think to become an American citizen. I never knew until earlier this month, when one of my friends finally was naturalized. She joined thirty-eight other Southwest Virginia residents who were persistent enough to take and pass the naturalization test – What did the Emancipation Proclamation do? Why did the Pilgrims come to America? What INS form is used to apply to become a naturalized citizen? – learn to read, write and speak English and wait five years until permanent residency was established. According to my friend, you really have to want to be a citizen to have the persistence it takes to follow up with the Bureau of Citizenship and Immigration Services.

But when you finally get that phone call that your paperwork has been approved, your tests have been passed and your English is comprehensible, then driving down to Roanoke's District court seems like an insignificant distance compared to how far you've really come.

My friend from Russia stood up there with five other Indians, two Canadians, one Swiss and three Iraqis to name a few. Citizenship to some immigrants means more than the right to vote, it means a different quality of life – anything from the freedom to walk down the street unaccompanied to faster checkout lines at the supermarket. Regardless, most of them stood up cheering, looking proud – and a few appeared relieved. I could only image their different reasons for coming, the different sacrifices they endured and the different dreams that may have been dancing in their heads.

A few rows behind were a pair of children wide-eyed and staring at a parent concentrating hard as she repeated the oath of citizenship. And as the judge proudly welcomed them as United States citizens, the kids jubilantly jumped up fiercely waving the familiar prize firmly attached to their hands – this time, an American flag.

© The Roanoke Times, Apr. 29, 2003, www.roanoke.com, by Krisha Chachra

Finding Your Dreams Where You Live

I couldn't have been the only kid that dreamed of running away from Blacksburg to be a movie star in California.

Late one afternoon I hopped on my pink banana seat bike determined to pedal my way into the lifestyle of the rich and famous. With the newest set of Crayola felt-tip markers tucked in the basket between the handlebars, I planned on making my living coloring my way across the country until I got to the West Coast. If I got short on cash, I'd sell my drawings and live off the endless supply of honeysuckle I'd plucked from my backyard, all finally in full bloom. It was a masterful plan that had taken all summer to calculate.

Full of momentum, I made it to the top of the hill. Just before I turned the corner to start my new adventure, I glanced back at my home. It was almost dinnertime and I knew my mom would be waiting for me. Maybe I'd humor her and have one more real meal before I embarked on my honeysuckle diet. I pedaled back, this time with another kind of hunger on my mind. California could wait until tomorrow.

We all have a few big dreams that are nothing more than just food for our imagination. Buddha says, "A child without dreams is like a night without stars." So who could blame us for reaching? In today's realm of 'reality' television, an American Idol is born every day. We see young adults, some with amazing presence – some hardly with any talent – dancing, acting, singing and sometimes embarrassing their way to the top overnight. Maybe it gives us confidence when we secretly say to ourselves that we could be there if we really wanted to be. But we choose not to be because that's just not our reality.

That kind of fame and attention is short lived and requires more work then we're probably willing to give. But we don't necessarily need the bright lights and big city to make big dreams come true. We can live them here in our small town of Blacksburg, because we're here – and here, unlike on TV – dreams seem to last.

After all, it was here, back when no one had computers in their homes, that Virginia Tech, Andrew Cohill and the rest of the BEV members had a wild dream to wire the community. That dream came true and our town became famous.

Blacksburg resident Lindsay West dreamed of bringing the Lyric Theatre back to life and sparked a movement that resulted in keeping this historical landmark open for movies, live performances and community events. Now the Lyric is famous and so is she.

We can't forget countless other people and organizations that started their dreams, lived them out or grew them while living in Blacksburg. The people of this town have cloned sheep, trained a NFL first round draft pick, inspired a community foundation, created their own companies, served their country, held public office, educated thousands of children and young adults, traveled the world, become wealthy opinion leaders, written best sellers and raised responsible kids.

There are plenty of us in this town that are in a comfortable transition period. We have a lot of grand ideas swimming around in our heads and think if only we could get out, then maybe our dreams could come true. But getting out only changes the focus of your dreams. Staying forces you to live them.

As it turns out, California never happened and neither did the movie star contract. But that's OK, because I tried the bright lights and big city some time ago and it changed my dream. I'm back now living in Blacksburg, the breeding ground where those dreams were first inspired. I plan on living them out; only this time, I'm not waiting for the honeysuckle to bloom.

© The Roanoke Times, Jun. 3, 2003, www.roanoke.com, by Krisha Chachra

Find Your Own Stories to Tell

Can't catch a break? Don't wait around for a vacation – take one, in your own backyard.

Sometimes, as young professionals in this town, our surroundings seem a little boring. But those of us who grew up here know that only a boring person gets bored in these parts.

Gov. Mark Warner declared that boosting tourism to Southwest Virginia is essential to the economic development of our area. But just like anything else, we have to know it before we sell it to outsiders. Sure, we could point passers-by to the scenic vistas of the Blue Ridge, or the serenity of Peaks of Otter, or maybe even the rapids of the James and New rivers.

But if you're a local, you know all that stuff is for the tourists – the real adventure lies behind the façade printed on the glossy brochure. Behind the thicket – now that's where the stories are.

I could tell so many, but then I'd be giving it all away. All the secret hideouts, the tracks where kids discover animal bones and the unmarked waterfall that guarantees the best setting for a first kiss. There are so many summertime adventures that unfold into classic stories for the ages, at least among your friends.

But I shouldn't say anything.
OK, maybe just one.

Take the legend of the chains on Fallen Branch Road. One foreboding eve, a gang of my high school friends piled in one of our parents' embarrassing family vehicles and winded back toward the woods across the street from Hills. Braving the sizzling summer drizzle and deep haze – which only added to the mysterious ambience – we stretched our necks out and rudely hushed at each other, concentrating to hear between the raindrops for the sound of rattling chains.

Legend has it that a runaway slave, bound by metal chains at the hands, fell in a hole somewhere in the acres behind the Long John Silver's in Christiansburg. He had died there, in the pouring rain, exhausted by his attempts to cut his chains off against a rock. Supposedly, when you go there, you can sometimes hear the clamor of his desperation – but only when it rains.

I heard it that night. Distinctive rhythmic pulses, back and forth like a swing-set. It was definitely metal on metal like the clatter a chain tied to a pole would make, hitting it against the wind. But this had a human element. It was like the fallen slave's ghost was banging his chains hard and then taking a break. We all heard it – one loud mother of a bang. And then, our screaming. Tearing down from the trees, we fell into the car and tore away, maybe only a hundred yards, before we dared ourselves to go back and find out the source of the noise. Later, one kid admitted to rigging a bike chain on a metal fence. No one believed him; no one wanted to.

It was fun, teasing each other, declaring "I ain't scared" and then being too scared to leave the car. Everyone at school talked about it, everyone went there that summer and everyone had their own stories to tell.

So if you haven't already been carried downstream out of the valley by the torrential storms of late, build your own ark and get out there. Go to McAfee's Knob, the Upper Falls, Mountain Lake, the local wineries, the Blue Ridge Parkway or even just in your own backyard. But wherever you go, make your own legends and find your own stories to tell. That's the real beauty of living in the Blue Ridge – sometimes it's not what you see, but what you can say about it. Yes, the mountains are pretty to look at, the waterfalls are romantic and the undulating landscapes make the best pictures. But nothing makes living here more picturesque than your own imagination.

© The Roanoke Times, Jul. 8, 2003, www.roanoke.com, by Krisha Chachra

The undulating ridges of the Blue Ridge Mountains. Photo © Ian J. Plant

Rain Makes Gardens, and Families, Grow?

Where have all these rabbits come from? I swear, there are more rodents and critters darting out in front of cars and nibbling on the garden than there were all last year. With the season's record rainfall creating mini landslides and flooding underground borrows, how could all of nature's creatures save themselves from drowning and also find the time to well, multiply?

The birds and the bees haven't been the only ones. In the midst of sweeping out flooded basements, repairing damaged gutters and being marooned indoors, it seems like several young couples I know in town have found themselves announcing "one on the way" this summer.

In general, my friends – I'll go even wider and say maybe my entire age group, minus a few high school comrades who found their soul mates early – had put marriage and starting a family on hold. Our careers needed advancing, our independence was too important and there were just too many things to accomplish and experience before getting tied down. Staying up all day and out all night was standard. Meeting new people and dating around was not required but just preferred. Case in point: a few 20-something locals and myself organized a social group called the New River Nucleus just to connect people with each other, so it wouldn't be so boring to live single and young in Blacksburg.

But suddenly, behind closed doors, it seems like a bunch of the crowd is settling down, secretly plotting how to change their lives to look more like their parents', without, of course, looking exactly like their parents'. Deep down, I guess we all want that American Dream that still includes a spouse, a house and 2.2 kids. Still, that thought was always someday in the future, and that future wasn't coming anytime soon.

So, how do we account for the recent shift in priorities? I blame it on the rain.

The weather has prevented me from seeing it coming. Outdoor barbecues and company picnics have been canceled because of rain, ironically, drying up the grapevine. Casual run-ins downtown where conversation about future plans are welcomed have been replaced with getting caught outside during a storm, blowing past an acquaintance, yelling "I'll call you" over your shoulder. Weather can easily be blamed for keeping out of touch, except with the people you live with. Pretty soon you're committing to live with them the rest of your life.

The results have been staggering. Besides the declarations to add additions to the family, I received nine wedding announcement emails with the subject "Save the Date," four full-fledged wedding invitations, two formal engagement party invites and one desperate phone call from a male friend of mine who can't decide whether or not to pop the question this summer.

Wait until the sun comes out and then see how you feel, was my advice.

But I suppose it makes sense. A marriage and a happy family, I've heard, like an attractive garden or lawn, needs considerable planning, attention and work. In between all the rainfall, the young couples have probably taken advantage of the opportunity to de-weed, prune and groom both their lawns and their relationships this season. And now, both entities look really appealing to come home to every day.

So maybe the goals for outdoor home improvement suffered a little this season, but it seems like some of us were still busy. Congratulations to all those couples who have made the storm work for their marriages and families. And for those who didn't get hitched or couldn't plan for a family this rainfall, don't worry. Lighten up and soak up all the sun you can get from what's left of the summer. When the time is right, I guarantee the rain will come again.

© The Roanoke Times, Aug. 12, 2003, www.roanoke.com, by Krisha Chachra

Goodbye Summer, Hello Student Hoards

I hate to admit this, but I'm finally at the age that I believe the summer is over when the students come back into town.

There. I've said it. The greatest confession of a local that goes unspoken year after year. We really do love the students – we know their value and their unmatchable importance to this town. There was even a time in high school when I couldn't wait to be one of them.

Back then, when the students returned to school with their double-parked hatchbacks, stuffed to the tops of the windows with crates of clothes, Blacksburg pulsed back to life. Kids would flood the intersections like party confetti, sporting the latest fashion trends, popping their gum, showing off their summer tans and squealing with excitement at the top of their lungs at the sight of each other.

They were back at school and so, so cool, and by the beginning of September this town went from a boring ghost town to having character again.

But now, somehow I'm just not so enamored of the new people that share my town come fall. Suddenly I miss not having to arrive early to find a place to park downtown; I have to concentrate extra hard when I drive around – the way home that I normally can maneuver with my eyes closed is now planted with unpredictable obstacles like youngsters stepping out in front of my car or cars braking in front of me so the driver can acknowledge his friends from the window. I don't like pushing my way through a crowd of tube-topped freshman at a local hangout that didn't get a second look from anyone all summer and hearing my favorite bartender tell me, "Girl, you gotta stand in line."

Stand in line? A few days ago I was part of the gang that kept this place in business. Forget it. This town is now a zoo. I don't even recognize it. I'll just go home – if I can get there without getting into an accident.

Admittedly, I'm probably just jealous. I remember how much fun it was to return to college at William and Mary, after a reckless summer of stories, and feel like you owned the place. This is a very old subject – the feeling of youthful immortality and wild energy is like walking around with blinders on. You really don't have the awareness or the concern for what you may be stepping into – even if it is an on-coming car. There is a history that includes people who have routines in place before you arrived, but you don't care – unless it has your name all over it.

But I digress. I suppose I feel so removed from those days of over-confidence because for the last five years I've been living in the real world where everyone has bright ideas, is equally as vocal and tries just as hard as everyone else. Being the loudest squealer doesn't cut it to get attention anymore. At least not the kind of attention you want.

And this is just in the last five years. In the last ten years, I've gone from admiring the cool college kids, leaving the town to become one of them (at least in theory) and then coming back to town just to realize I can't handle them anymore. And that, my friends, sadly, means we're just old. So old that this summer my Blacksburg high school friends asked me to help plan our 10-year reunion.

Ten years? I never thought I would be this "old." I don't feel like that much time has passed. Our first meeting was more of a catch-up session. Who has married whom. How many kids do they have? Has anyone been divorced? How can you plan a reunion that will be fun for the money-making professionals, struggling grad students and responsible parents all at the same time? That's a topic for a future column. But the point is that no matter what we decide to do for our reunion weekend, we'll own the town again – at least for that moment.

Now, where the heck did I stash my tube top?

© The Roanoke Times, Sep. 16, 2003, www.roanoke.com, by Krisha Chachra

Driven to Distraction on I-81

I was wrong. Working and living in the New River Valley really can skew your sense of distance. If you live around the end of North Main Street, for instance, you'll never do any last-minute shopping at a Kroger – while it's just a few miles away, the University City Boulevard grocery store is simply too far. Food Lion is your best bet to tide you over until the weekend, when you finally have enough time to pile everyone in the car to make that ritual family trip to the mall area, a whole 10 minutes away. For those of us living on the south side of town, the weekend trip to Wal-Mart takes only five minutes. The bypass, my friends, has changed our lives.

Sadly, my battles aren't with downtown stoplights anymore – now I worry about being trapped in a sandwich dance between two 18-wheelers down Christiansburg Mountain. Don't get me wrong, my 1996 Honda Civic can hold its own on the highway, but I can see why most of my friends reserve the nerve-wracking drive to the Star City for infrequent rock concerts at the civic center. But what can I do? My opportunity is there, and I do love the energy and events in the city once I arrive. But the drive – well, I've learned to deal.

At first I used the 40 minutes to catch up on phone calls (don't worry, I use an ear piece). But when a monster truck is chasing your tail and a cop is waiting for you to make a wrong move, you're too distracted to keep the conversation going.

So I started to just pay more attention to the road. Now my commute

goes like this: From the ramp merging onto I-81 north, I see to the right the model log home that someday I want to own. A few miles down, I squeeze my brakes down to 65 mph as I anticipate seeing our local law enforcement car tucked behind a mound in the median, his secret hideaway. I'm on to him and I wave as I drive by.

Soon I veer to the left and I'm at exit 128. A burst of fall color – the sun is in my face now, the sky is electric blue, trees blaze with hard reds and piercing oranges cradled by a base of warm browns. It is an eyeful, and the best part of my trip as of yet, but the exit is a landmark in itself. As I pass by, I remember the little pizza place farther off the exit where my homecoming date took me for dinner. He was being adventurous, but at the time, I just thought he was a cheapskate. Now I would consider a date at Mountain View Italian Kitchen a novelty. He was way beyond his years.

Right after that is the only rest stop on my way. Knowing it is now or never if I need to go, I drive past – I can make it, I only have about 14 miles left. At the home stretch there is a straightaway, just before mile marker 137, where the speed limit drops to 60. That's when all the other cars fly by me. Novices.

But the landmark just before this is what interests me. I see it: the place that made me think of days when driving down I-81 meant I was going on vacation. As a kid peering out of the window of my family's car, passing Richfield Retirement Home meant we were close to the airport. I would get excited when I spotted that pale building, knowing that pretty soon I'd be taking off, going somewhere.

And now, as I pass it alone in my car heading toward the studio in pursuit of my dream, in a different way, I hope it still means the same thing.

© The Roanoke Times, Oct. 21, 2003, www.roanoke.com, by Krisha Chachra

Give Thanks for Family, Food, and Football

Thanksgiving was always one of the most anticipated holidays for me growing up in this turkey town.

Taking the exit off 64 West to Interstate 81 South from Williamsburg, where I attended college, I'd see my Hokie counterparts heading the opposite direction, hatchbacks stuffed with laundry bags, going to Northern Virginia for the holidays. Good. Blacksburg would be left to the local turkeys by the time I'd reach exit 118. It would be a reunion of high school friends at PK's and some good Southern cooking.

Well, Southern Indian cooking in my case. But still, something to be thankful for.

And then, there were other things about Thanksgiving at home that just couldn't be replaced. Football was one of them. We'd huddle around the big screen to watch the classic Redskins vs. Cowboys match-up. And while my mom yelled from the kitchen for my brother and me to set the table, we'd ignore her and talk about what we considered to be the 'good old Gibbs days' for the 'Skins – the Monk, Sanders, Clark era. What had happened to the formidable force of 'The Posse' that reigned during our childhood?

It was so great to come home and talk football: not only pro football, but college football, too. Granted, William and Mary was a great school and I went there for the academics, but man, I missed Hokie sports. Football season without energy like we had here in Blacksburg was a painful experience. But after a while, you learn to do without, and when I'd return to school each fall season I would learn to redirect my spirit to supporting another kind of football that William and Mary excelled in: soccer.

Before I graduated, Redskins owner Jack Kent Cooke died, and two years after that, the team that had made Thanksgiving such an event in our living room was sold to some 30 year-old multimillionaire named Synder. How can I explain? It just wasn't the same.

But that same year, 1999, Hokie football was perfect. That sweet sugar converted into energy for me again as we hungrily followed our team down in New Orleans. It wasn't just the game. I had missed the scene, the reunion with friends, the crowds of celebrating, passionate people and the juicy stories afterward.

I was back.

Even though I lived in the nation's capital, a new fan of D.C. United Soccer (an interest left over from my William and Mary days) and had gotten over my disappointment with the Redskins, there was no question: Just scratching the surface, you could tell I was still a Hokie fan. A Blacksburg fan. A hometown supporter. And I was thankful for it.

So this week, be thankful too. For anything and everything that never really left you, that still feeds energy to your soul, and reminds you of a good place like home. It might be exit 118, family, friends or food. And, don't be afraid to admit it: Living in this town, you gotta be thankful for football.

© The Roanoke Times, Nov. 25, 2003, www.roanoke.com, by Krisha Chachra

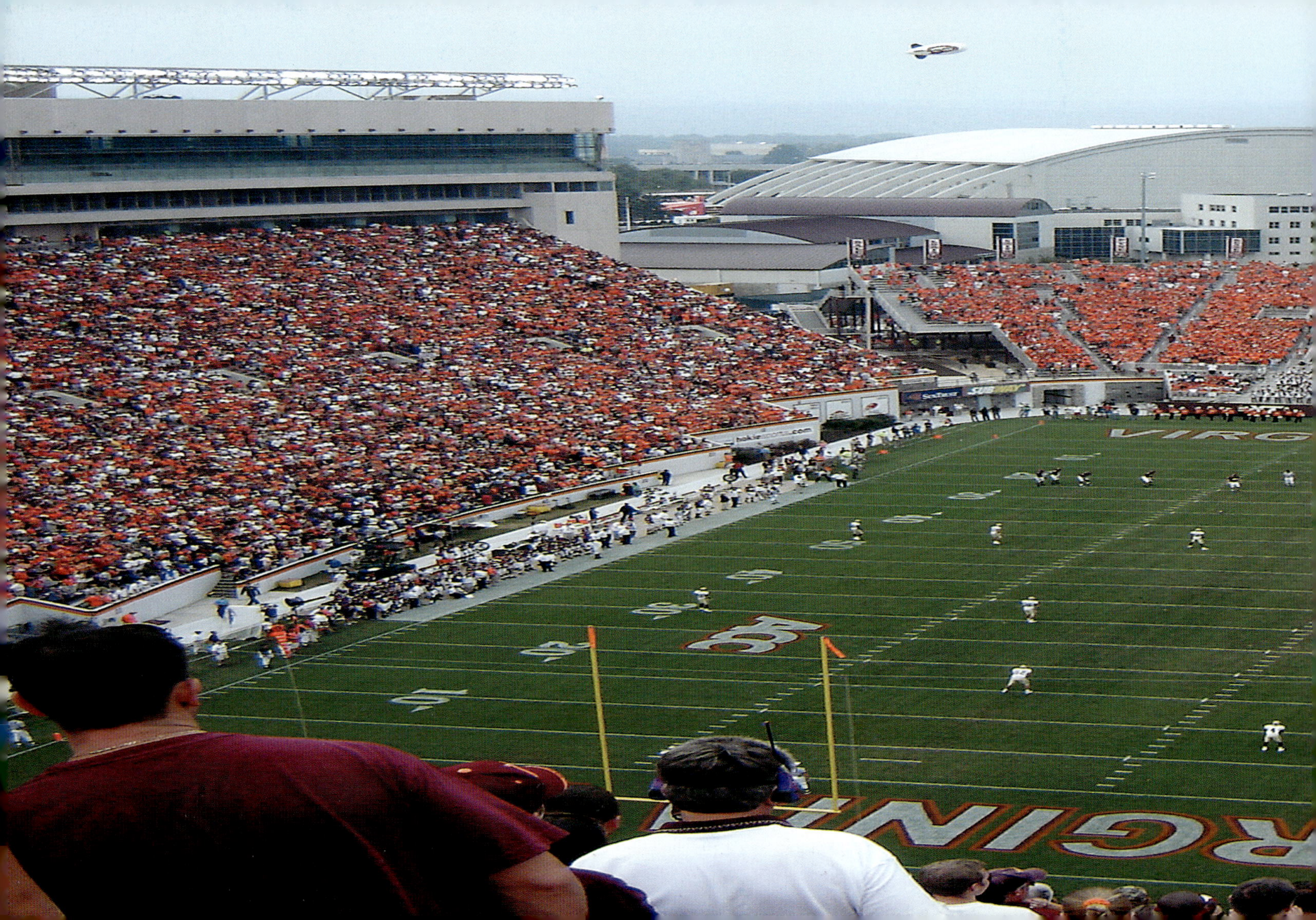
VIRG
SUBWAY

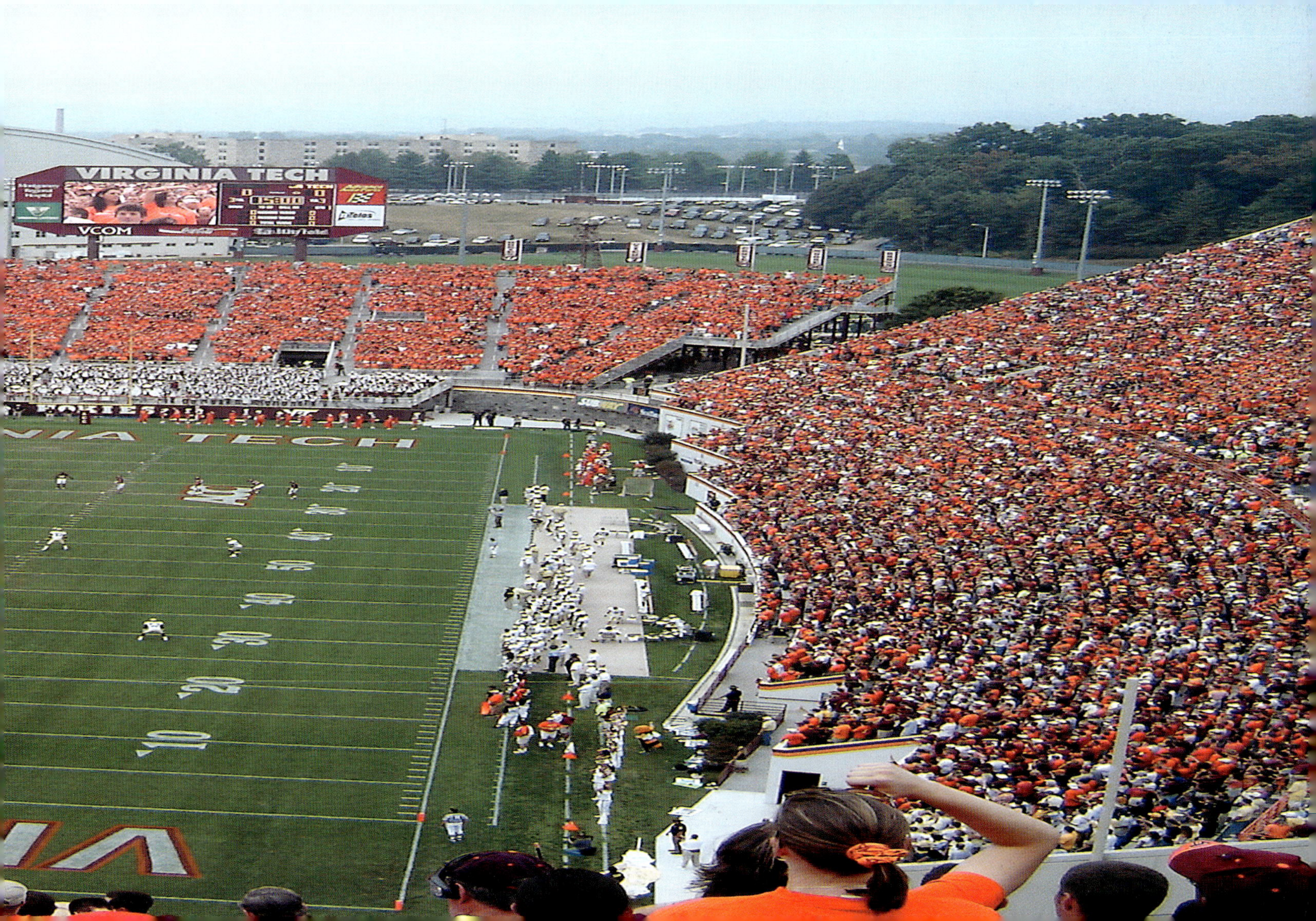
VIRGINIA TECH
VCOM

Blacksburg is Always Just a Memory Away

Looking out from my window seat, the New River Valley was only a speck among the patchwork of houses and mountains below. My final destination, Rio de Janeiro, Brazil, was 12 hours away, and trying to find a landmark to bid farewell to my hometown was the least I could do as I left the winter behind.

But leaving the weather was the obvious part. It's the reminders of my hometown, especially the people, that never seem to escape me no matter where in the world I land.

When you travel overseas, where you come from suddenly becomes important. In Southeast Asia, meeting a person from Michigan means an instant connection. Sharing a cab with a person from Virginia forms a true brotherly friendship. Sometimes the irony is too stark: Travel halfway around the world just to meet someone who lives or once lived in your back yard. But it happens to me, and I'm sure to many others. Even when you aim to get away, somehow a piece of home finds you and reminds you that coming back actually won't be as hard as it seems.

Not even a year ago, my mom and dad were taking a funicular in the Alps when a friendly Swiss couple advised them to stay on for an extra stop to see a spectacular view. They started chatting with the locals and exchanged small talk about where they were from. My mom explained that our family was from a university town in Virginia in the United States.

Figuring that was more than enough detail for their new friends, she continued the conversation of pleasantries as the next stop approached. Sitting nearby on the train, another woman, who was obviously eavesdropping, lowered her newspaper and interrupted my mother with, "You're talking about Blacksburg, aren't you? I love that place!"

Shocked that a random Swiss stranger on her Alpine adventure had pinpointed the New River Valley as though it was the most obvious location in the world that my parents could have hailed from, my mom recovered quickly. "Yes, actually that is where we are from," she said. "How did you know?"

The Swiss woman knew because she had once visited the New River Valley and soon felt she fit in enough to call Blacksburg her second home.

And she is not the only person that my family has met on our overseas travels who has had the same feelings for our area and its people.

Blacksburgians make quite an impression on our visitors – not to mention, we do a great deal of traveling ourselves. We might be strongly opinionated about the looks of our new parking garage downtown or the question of whether we can legally commemorate a bridge to our longtime mayor who still happens to be in office, but our interests don't end there. People from Blacksburg and the rest of the New River Valley make their mark on a global scale, which makes our small corner of the world, well, kind of famous. We teach students in foreign countries, advance research by engaging in international partnerships, publish studies in different languages, journey to exotic locations and simply extend friendship to an international visitor who never forgets how special this place and the people are.

It is exciting that you never quite know who you're going to meet when you travel. But it is comforting to know the kind of people you're always going to return home to.

© The Roanoke Times, Feb. 3, 2004, www.roanoke.com, by Krisha Chachra

When the Past Emerges Out of the Soggy Present

Last month a homeowner's biggest nightmare happened to my parents. Their basement flooded. Boxes upon boxes holding decades of memories and forgotten secrets were dampened and blurred over with the weight of water. It was a mess for them to clean up, but slowly each box was examined, contents kept aside or discarded, one after another.

Opening each box was like Christmas, my mom said – a damaged wet lid lifted to uncover lost loot. I have no idea why she ever kept some of those things.

Baby clothes that I once loved – too cute to throw out, but too outdated for any modern hip kid to wear – were squeezed out and hung to dry. Old blankets that collected more dust than they ever gave warmth were saved. And most importantly, she discovered my old sticker albums, which framed the world's most prized unicorn and wiggly-eyed stickers.

I remember I traded four coveted rainbow stickers for a huge velvet heart that I used to tuck safely in the book, with the waxy paper still on its back to preserve the adhesive. Now, the most beautiful sticker known to man was soaked at the bottom of the box, never once used to accent a letter or seal an envelope. What a waste. Why did I ever keep it hidden?

And then all those notebooks, textbooks, and piles and piles of essays. The words that I slaved over to structure the perfect sentence and convey the perfect thought were now stuck together, incomprehensible. I flipped through my statistics notebook and couldn't believe I had been an econ major in college. How did I ever solve that problem? I don't even know what those variables mean anymore.

At least the entire collection of AP History themes, corrected and approved by my high school American History teacher Delores Grapsas, wasn't ruined. I couldn't even tell you who Lord North was anymore but apparently I had written an entire essay about him. I guess keeping all those papers proved I actually knew important things at one time.

My parents also shared objects they had saved from their first years in this foreign country. Old saris that my mom wore as a school teacher during her first job, in Fredericksburg. My dad's "Speak Up" award from his Blacksburg Jaycees days. Old wedding invitations and napkins for a marriage that happened thousands of miles away from their families now were drying out on the basement table.

And then my mom showed me a salvaged letter. It smelled like mold and looked older than me. It was, actually, seven years older than me, sent in 1969 to my grandmother by her wonderstruck daughter who was living a dream in America. "Momma," my mother wrote, "you'll never believe what they have here – drive up windows at the bank. You can sit at your car, write a cheque [sic] and get money right there at the window. It is so easy!" It was humbling; my mom was so amazed by the convenience of the modern Western world and couldn't wait to share her new discoveries with her mother in India.

But the irony of finding the letter was that not even a month before the flooding, my mom had received an email from my brother who had given her a lesson of how times had changed. "Mom," he typed in a reaction to her asking if he'd balanced his checkbook that month, "only stone-age people balance their accounts on a check register. I look up my balance practically everyday online."

We laughed at the comparison. My mom kept that email just as she'd kept the recovered letter sent to her mother in 1969. I suppose that is how the past becomes the present – from the wishes, words and wonders that float to the surface when the water rushes in.

© The Roanoke Times, Mar. 9, 2004, www.roanoke.com, by Krisha Chachra

Would Founding Family be Proud of this Town?

If William Black could see his town now, what would he think?

In 1798, William Black, son of Irish immigrant Samuel Black, established the village of Blacksburg, consisting of 38 acres of land.

Ever wonder why the Town of Blacksburg's logo is a four-by-four square pattern turned 45 degrees? Well, that was William's original arrangement for the layout of the village: a grid creating 16 blocks where community buildings were placed strategically throughout. About a hundred years later, one of the founder's descendents, Alexander Black, erected the elegant Victorian house that, 50 years later, became the funeral parlor we all knew on Main Street. And about 60 years after that, my friend and I sat watching from a window seat in Backstreets Pizza as they moved that historic Black House across the street to Draper Road.

Things have surely shifted, to say the least. Back then land in the original 16-square downtown area could probably be purchased for what we would consider to be peanuts now. But try buying a house in Blacksburg today. Even with the interest rates at rock bottom, young professionals like me can hardly afford to purchase a starter home in our own town. Real estate is so expensive in Blacksburg today that several of our local young investors who want to stay in this town have to look in Christiansburg or Radford or even move out to Roanoke. Slowly they settle in, have families and raise kids that attend schools in other districts. If they save enough and keep their Blacksburg ties, maybe one day they will be able move back. But if not, their offspring, not to mention their tax dollars, go elsewhere.

And it is not only the young people of Blacksburg that are feeling the squeeze – a 25-year Blacksburg resident and friend of mine recently joked that if he put his house on the market today, he wouldn't even be able to afford to buy it himself.

So what would the Black family say today?

Would they be appalled at the rapid growth that has made it unaffordable for some locals to even live here anymore? Would they be floored that their little 16-plot village transformed into the innovative electronic village? Or maybe they would be confused as to how the new stop light on Clay Street was installed to ease the flow of downtown traffic but had the reverse effect of backing it up for 15 extra minutes. What would they say about the current sewer controversy that has resulted with a few locals suing the town?

And finally, what would they think about their elaborate Victorian house that was moved across the street to make way for a parking lot?

I suppose a hundred years from now, it will make little difference where the Black House used to be. In fact, this week Blacksburg residents will be remarking on new historical changes like how the five new owners of Bogen's restaurant decided to scrap their signature monopoly style menu but opted to keep their famous wafto fries. Or that Long John Silver's is now a locally owned restaurant called Lefty's, a tribute to all the high profiled left-handed people of the world (including the owner – a new-comer from Los Angeles).

What will matter is that even though the town progressed, it preserved its original character and compassion. Maybe we'll see that Bill Ellenbogen left his restaurant business to smartly develop subdivisions and protect the wooded beauty of this area. That even though we attracted an Outback or an Applebee's, homegrown restaurants like Lefty's, Vincent's and Souvlaki's can still survive. And when Kent Square is fully operational, finally relieving the downtown parking congestion, we can walk around the block to see the old Alexander Black house, moved from its original location, just to be fully restored and converted into the Blacksburg Museum and Cultural Services Facility.

Now that's a town William Black would be proud of.

© The Roanoke Times, Apr. 13, 2004, www.roanoke.com, by Krisha Chachra

From My Shadow to My Friend

At first, dealing with newcomers can be such a drag.

A quarter of a century ago last week, a newcomer came out of nowhere and into my life. He was kinda small, not really interesting, and lifeless. Yet somehow he attracted more attention upon his arrival than I ever remember getting. I didn't really understand what the fuss was all about; it was not like he could play, color or say anything worthwhile. My dad lifted me up so I could peer through thick glass to see him. Apparently this newcomer was my little brother.

I was 3 and the world revolved around me. I was my daddy's girl and my mommy's pride and joy – the first-born American in my family's history. We would picnic at the duck pond, and I would generously throw whole slices of bread before learning that ducks preferred small balled-up pieces. I must have accidentally fallen in that duck pond at least twice before the newcomer arrived; an accidental Duck Pond dunk is pretty much an initiation for every Blacksburg local who grew up here. When we weren't at the pond, we'd be playing checkers on the Drillfield or running wild at the caboose park.

The first years of my life, my parents tried their best to raise me in a country still foreign to them without the help, supervision or guidance from their families halfway around the world. A dream-come-true situation, some might say, but I'm sure my parents would have gladly welcomed the somewhat intrusive "expert" advice from family members. Especially when it came to taming me.

It is legend in our household that by the time I could stand I was pulling myself over the confiding walls of the playpen. My mom had to place soft pillows around the perimeter to break my fall. I loved exploring my surroundings – sticking my hands in pot soil, pulling open cabinet doors, learning to scoot down stairs. My parents baby-proofed the entire house, but that only created a challenge, not a roadblock. By the time I could walk I would take off, leaving my parents in the dust with mild heart attacks. But I was just a curious kid. Fear of traffic, or punishment for that matter, never fazed me. My folks had what they never expected, a true American, free as a bird.

So when the newcomer came along I thought I would have a partner in crime or at least a distraction for those two pairs of vigilant eyes that always seemed to burn my back. But instead of two pairs of eyes to dodge, I got three. My brother was mesmerized, entertained by my every move. He rarely got up from his sitting position, too cautious to join me in my dance of disobedience in front of the adults.

Like a true younger sibling, he idolized my actions and mimicked my words. When I discovered the microphone and recorded stories of our family vacations, he would get his turn and tell the same story in exactly the same way. When I told him his favorite color was green, he told everyone proudly his favorite color was green. When I would run to be first in the school bus line, he would stand contentedly behind me as second in line. He even told me one day that his lucky number was two.

But like all newcomers, my brother soon acclimated. He started hanging out with his own friends and making his own stories to tell around town. The Drillfield was for the older, scholarly students, so his boys discovered "the bowl" in Hethwood to play ball in. The caboose park was so old school; they had the cool castle-like towers and walkways of the Hand-in-Hand playground to sneak around in. Although he did still fall in, the duck pond was a has-been hangout, full of families and lazy fowl. Instead, when he was old enough, his

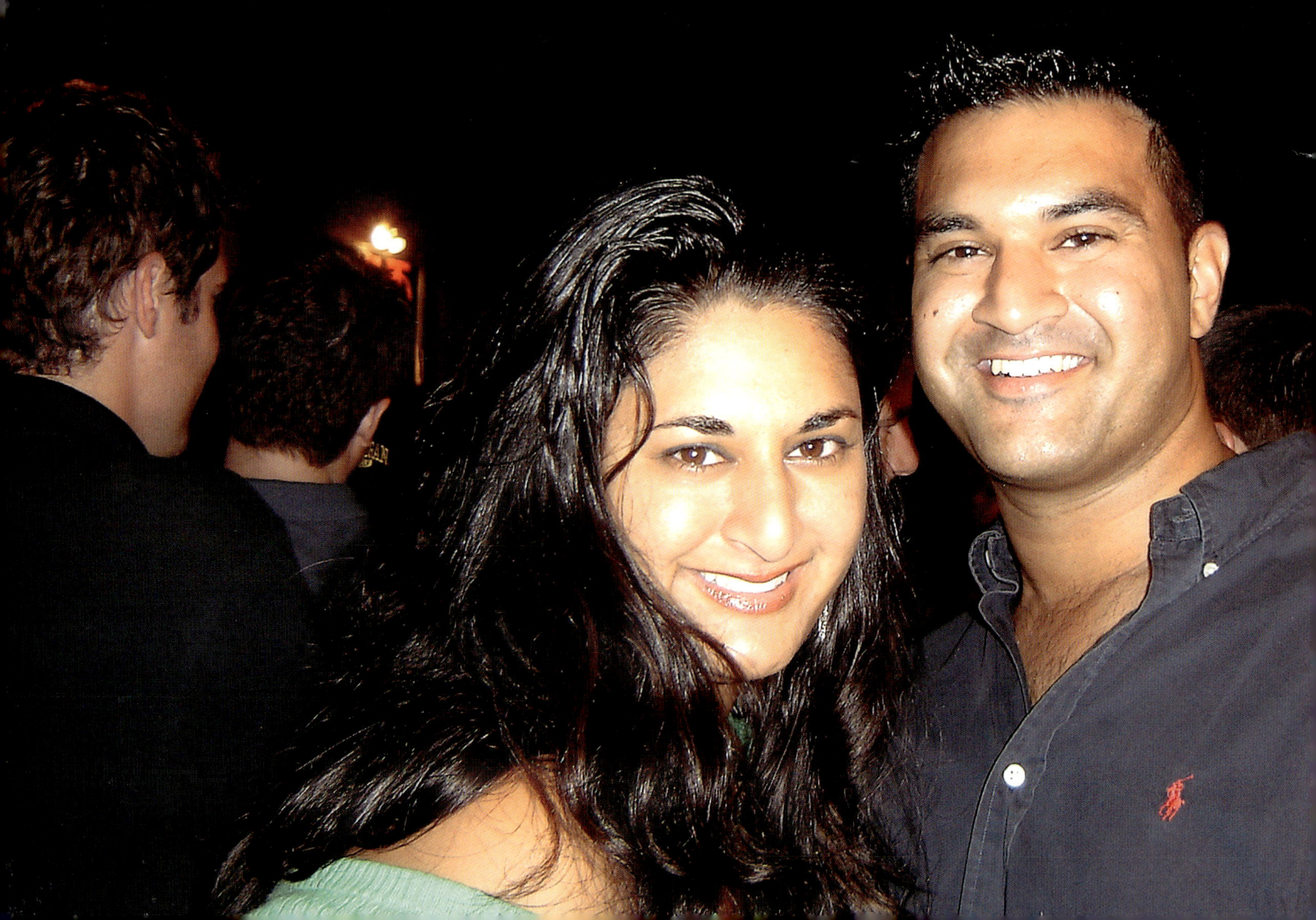

buddies would take him to spend summer weekends at Smith Mountain Lake. It was much cooler to jet ski than to throw bread.

And slowly he emerged from the back of the line to being on the front line of the BHS football team and the ringleader in his band of boys. He was never in anyone's shadow ever again. In fact, everyone around him seemed to be in his light. He was no longer my follower. Instead, he transformed into my friend. Over time, he really grew up in this town – in his own clever little way.

After 25 years, my brother is no newcomer to Blacksburg. In fact, each time he drives into town, he is shocked by the updates. The duck pond has a gazebo and new landscaping, the deteriorating Hand-in-Hand playground isn't as cool as the hip half pipe next to it, and Torgersen Hall Bridge now frames the mighty entrance to campus and the Drillfield. I suppose, he tells me, if you are open to new things, you start to appreciate them as they grow on you.

He doesn't know just how right he is.

© The Roanoke Times, May 19, 2004, www.roanoke.com, by Krisha Chachra

The Indians are Gathering for their 10th Reunion

It has been 10 years since I have officially been a Blacksburg Indian. But this weekend, I'll be reuniting with my tribe.

That first landmark anniversary is upon us. All graduates of Blacksburg High School's class of 1994 will descend on what we knew as the Balcony – now called Top of the Stairs – Friday night to begin a weekend long exchange of colorful stories and innocent embellishments about how the last 10 years have unfolded for us.

It has been in the making for almost a year now. Should we have a band or a DJ? Who should be the guest speaker? Should we show the senior slide show – that somewhat silly VHS tape that forever enshrined who was popular and cool enough to make it on camera. Who would come? Should we send invitations and make programs? Where were we going to get the resources?

In the end, our reunion committee, or the Fab Five as I'd like to call us now, realized that we had the resources to pull off a 10-year reunion right there within our group. One of our committee members had started his own advertising agency and could convert the VHS senior slide show into a DVD to sell on-site. Another member had strong ties to Virginia Tech and could secure a venue for our dinner and dance at the Donaldson Brown Center. I worked part-time at a high-tech company and could find someone to design our Web site. Forget paper invitations, we were living in the age of electronic registration and creating online directories. The way we gather information had changed in 10 years.

But we never could have anticipated the kind of information our fellow classmates would report to us when they registered. So many had married, becoming parents. Some had changed jobs several times, started their own companies, were still finishing college.

We had a few that moved to California, Colorado and New York – one as far away as Japan. One guy, who had taken Mr. Kaylor's photography class, had become a photographer and lived in India. Our homecoming queen had become a lawyer practicing in

Maryland. Our star women's basketball player found her calling as a professional referee. Another friend had graduated earlier and spent seven years in Israel. The guy who was named "Most Likely to be on the Cover of Rolling Stone" was a veterinarian – we weren't sure if he still played the guitar. The girl who was most likely to "Save the Bay" was moving to Gabon, Africa. One of our glamorous Laurel Chain attendants had become a financial planner at IBM.

Not many people knew that one of the quieter girls in high school was now managing an Olympic hopeful in Maryland. Deep sadness had turned into strength for one of our track runners who had lost her sister to cancer last year and now was running a marathon to raise money for leukemia and lymphoma in her honor. Who would have guessed that a mechanical engineer who we knew had designed hydrogen-powered cars had chucked his job and was sailing through the Caribbean islands on his 37-foot sailboat? Or that another girl who had always loved horses was featured in a novel that chronicles her life as a groom, the person responsible for every nuance of the horse's care, health, and spirit?

We were all spread out, like the stars we had become across the sky. And this one reunion would bring us all together.

I thought back to the times before the mascot had become a controversy. I had always been proud of being an Indian on two counts: I was born to parents from India but I grew up as a Blacksburg Indian, cheering on the football team, editing the school newspaper and attending the school dances. I used to joke about when my mom would receive PTA letters in the mail from the middle school that were titled "Dear Indian" and I would laugh thinking, "how did they know?"

So, of course, when the mascot changed to the Bruins, I could no longer look forward to those appropriately addressed letters in the mail. Sadly, I was one of the last remaining graduates who could still accurately call myself a Blacksburg Indian – but I know this weekend, no matter what the graduates of Blacksburg High School call themselves now, the class of 1994 are the real Blacksburg Indians, and we are back.

© The Roanoke Times, Jun. 22, 2004, www.roanoke.com, by Krisha Chachra

Columnist Ready to Spread her Wings on the Big Island

There is nothing I loathe more than packing up my life in cardboard boxes for a big move. OK, one thing: unpacking the boxes and discovering the junk I somehow deemed worth enough to carry to my new place.

It is an opportunity I can't pass up, and much to my parents' dismay (but at the same time, to their delight), I am moving away from my hometown – at least temporarily. To their dismay, I have chosen the farthest place possible from them while still remaining in the United Sates. To their delight, that place happens to be their favorite vacation spot: Hawaii.

It was four years ago that I returned to the New River Valley after college and graduate school in Washington, D.C. The move back to the southwest part of the state was supposed to be transitional – I was only back home awaiting job responses and getting a little experience in my field of study. After surviving 18 years of this place, I wasn't about to get comfortable with the idea of spending longer here than I had to. I hardly bought any new furniture, let alone cracked open a packed box.

Looking back, I don't understand why I felt returning home was synonymous with failure. Maybe it was the questions I got: "Oh, so you're back now?" or "What are you doing back?" followed by glances that read, "I guess you couldn't cut it in the real world away from home, huh?" These questions, of course, were posed by adults who watched me grow or who had kids my age who would rather live on the streets than face the shame of coming back.

In general, the insinuations are enough to keep returning young locals cooped up in their homes, dodging those summertime concerts on the hill across from the Lyric when the entire town comes out, ostensibly to "hear music" but really to scout behind their dark shades to see who's back.

Even if Sept. 11 had not happened that following year, I would like to think that I would have chosen to stay anyway. Through these columns in the New River Journal, I have tried to convey just how lucky I am to be from here. It is a realization I have arrived at only because I gave it time and embraced where I was from rather than rejecting it.

OK, so it took sometime to get used to hosting pig-pickings instead of cocktail parties. Or having to only walk around one block to check out the local nightlife.

But in the end, life was better. I, like so many other happy 20-somethings in this town, made the place work for me. I treasured the five-minute drive to work and used the extra time I would have wasted on commuting to learn how to make soap, teach a YMCA class, take yoga, read a book, practice reporting news for radio and television and get to know my parents at a different level. I tried to involve myself in our community and put time into things I felt were important, including helping create a young professionals group called the New River Nucleus. Reconnecting with high school friends and widening the circle to include new ones solidified friendships for life. Out exploration extended outside Blacksburg, touring wineries on the parkway, outdoor clubs on the lake, theaters in Southside, the racetrack in Danville and the restaurants in Roanoke.

Even before the downtown improvement project started, I felt the town had improved immensely. But it was probably because I saw this place in a different light – as a launching pad for new adventure. And when I got my start in my dream career of journalism through WVTF and Blue Ridge Public Television, those same adults started telling me, "Oh, I'm so glad you came back!" and "I bet your parents are so proud to have you doing well in your career here," followed by glances that read, "I wish my kids would come back closer to home, too."

I am so proud to be from Blacksburg. I cannot tell you how much I have appreciated so many of you encouraging me in my work and my writing. It is only in a place like this that your community feels like an extension of you family. So I'm packing my boxes, each sealed with some little thing that reminds me of the last four years here. I can say with confidence that I know those keepsakes are worthy enough to carry to my new place. I'm not leaving my memories behind; I'm taking them with me.

© The Roanoke Times, Jul. 27, 2004, www.roanoke.com, by Krisha Chachra

About the Author

Krisha Chachra is a columnist, podcaster, and writer from Blacksburg, Virginia. She has written a series of entertainment columns focusing on communication skills in the social, dating and relationships scene. Her work has appeared in Bella Magazine, The Roanoke Times, Honolulu Advertiser, USA Weekend Magazine and several online journals. She also hosted a live, call-in, daily television show on public television and reported and hosted segments for National Public Radio affiliates in Virginia and Hawaii. She has traveled to over 35 countries in 6 continents compiling human-interest stories for publication and works with international software company, VTLS Inc. in addition to writing her columns. Krisha holds a BA from William & Mary and a MA from American University. She most recently lived in Honolulu, HI where she taught communication courses at Hawaii Pacific University. Please contact her at krisha@vtls.com or visit her web site at www.socialtalkers.com